A Caregiver's Tips:
My Wife had Alzheimer's Disease

Story by Fred Buse
Co-Author: Marie Mayer

Fred Buse and his late wife Dot

Author's Tranquility Press
ATLANTA, GEORGIA

Copyright © 2024 by Fred Buse | Marie Mayer

All rights reserved. No part of this publication may be reproduced, distributed or transmitted in any form or by any means, including photocopying, recording, or other electronic or mechanical methods, without the prior written permission of the publisher, except in the case of brief quotations embodied in critical reviews and certain other noncommercial uses permitted by copyright law. For permission requests, write to the publisher, addressed "Attention: Permissions Coordinator," at the address below.

Fred Buse | Marie Mayer
Author's Tranquility Press
3900 N Commerce Dr. Suite 300 #1255
Atlanta, GA 30344
www.authorstranquilitypress.com

Ordering Information:
Quantity sales. Special discounts are available on quantity purchases by corporations, associations, and others. For details, contact the "Special Sales Department" at the address above.

A Caregiver's Tips: My Wife had Alzheimer's Disease
Hardback: 978-1-966088-34-9
Paperback: 978-1-966088-35-6
eBook: 978-1-966088-36-3

ACKNOWLEDGEMENT

I wish to thank Dr Leroy Gerchman and the staff at West End Medical Center in Allentown, PA, for their guidance during the nine-year course of my wife, Dot's, Alzheimer's odyssey.

Thanks to Hospice Saint John of Allentown, PA, and my neighbor, Gail Shanahan, who helped to care for Dot the last two weeks of her life and to friends who helped edit this story.

Special thanks to Marie Mayer, who co-authored the text, organized Tips, advised me to remove all extraneous details, and encouraged me to publish my story.

INTRODUCTION

The purpose in writing this account is to share experiences, ideas, and any insight gained as a caregiver coping with the long journey of caring for a parent, spouse or loved one.

Each patient is different and each caregiver's experience is different, but loss is the common denominator. As needs intensify you will be living two lives, your life and the patient's. You will experience every day as a physical, emotional, and mental challenge that demands total dedication on the part of the caregiver who chooses to care for the loved one at home.

The caregiver does this because of love and caring, mindful of the dignity of the patient even during trying times. You must be open-minded, patient, and understanding, refrain from quick reactions to difficult behaviors, and accept changes. A patient's mind may forget the present and revert to past experiences which are totally foreign to you, perhaps even who you are. Eventually care seems to become overwhelming and unending. You will be tested, but the care you give because of love will see you through.

My hope is that the 134 tips included in this personal story as a caregiver may help other caregivers who choose to keep their loved one at home. To choose to do so is one of the most physically, mentally and challenging tasks anyone will ever encounter that demands total dedication on the part of the caregiver.

Each chapter highlights tips for caregivers about legal matters, Social Security, progress of the disease, patient behaviors, adjustments to daily life, hygiene, food and meals, medications, Hospice care, preparing for the demise, memorial services, and after death issues.

Contents

Go to Page 53 for content details of each chapter

Introduction iv

Chapter 1
  Onset of the Disease 1

Chapter 2
  Adjustments 15

Chapter 3
  Progression of the Disease 31

Chapter 4
  Medication 37

Chapter 5
  Going Home 43

CHAPTER 1
Onset of the Disease

Background

I was raised on the south shore of Long Island, New York, and graduated as a marine engineer from New York State Maritime College in 1958. I then accepted a position at Ingersoll Rand as an application engineer. In 1960 I married Dot Smith who was a secretary at Ingersoll Rand. We were married by Pastor Warren Harding in 1960 and vowed "in sickness and health, until death do us part". We had a happy marriage and then in 1997 Dot was diagnosed with Alzheimer's disease.

Alzheimer Disease

I noticed that Dot's short-term memory was starting to fail considerably. Our family doctor, after a thorough examination, suspected Alzheimer's disease and recommended we consult with a neurologist, who confirmed the diagnoses. Aricept was prescribed in hopes of slowing the progress of the disease.

Tip: *If dementia is suspected consult your family doctor immediately and request a second opinion.*

Legal protection

I chose to retire in 2000 to care for my wife. At that time we consulted our attorney to set up our estate, wills, living wills, power of attorney and other financial matters. I realized if something happened to me, provisions had to be established to protect Dot and the estate. When a medical hardship occurs anyone could be confronted with the responsibility of the person who has dementia. Rather than burden an individual we chose to set up a trust with the bank. Upon the bank's recommendation, I consulted a lawyer who specializes in trust accounts. A joint account was kept open so Dot's Social Security check could still be deposited. A new account solely in my name was opened and the majority of other funds were deposited. The basis was in case of my demise no probate is necessary; the trust would kick in and be managed by the bank. The bank would find a suitable facility for Dot, pay monthly bills to the facility and other estate bills. This decision was a big relief to all.

> **Tip**: *Establish legal documents to protect the patient and estate. Consult with a lawyer regarding trust, wills, living wills and power of attorney.*
> **Tip**: *Power-of-attorney is very important; it gives your appointed person the authority to take care of your affairs.*
> **Tip**: *Do not wait until the person cannot understand what is being done or cannot sign their name.*

Bills

Dot had fallen and hurt her leg, which was X-rayed. I received a bill. Upon closer examination I realized the billing reflected X-rays done for her shoulder and arm injured in a fall the year before. I was confused and called the billing department and told them that Dot's leg had been X-rayed, but the billing stated it was for x-rays of her shoulder. The person reviewed the statement and said the invoice was for X-rays done the previous year for the arm and shoulder, not the more recent X-rays for the leg injury. I was surprised to learn that billing agents are allowed 18 months to submit a bill to the provider, so I was careful to check dates thereafter.

> **Tip**: *Keep careful records of medical charges and dates when services are rendered.*

Social Security, Pension taxes, Medicare

I thought, naively, that you kept the entire Social Security amount after signing up for benefits, but discovered one must pay taxes and that Medicare was deducted also from the benefits. The bank can set up an account to automatically put a percentage of one's Social Security to save for taxes. I learned that taxes are due on pension plans also.

> **Tip**: *After retirement taxes are due from Social Security and pension benefits. Medicare is deducted automatically from Social Security.*

Support organizations

I found seminars sponsored by the local Alzheimer's society to be helpful. They provided information for the caregiver and the family, such as assisted living homes, day care availability, Alzheimer's units and caregiver hotlines.

> **Tip**: *Avail yourself of the services and support that agencies provide. The local Alzheimer's society sponsors seminars and caregiver hotlines.*

Changes

The patient may repeat the same question or conversation over and over, which eventually may become very annoying to the listener, and anyone else within close proximity.

A friend who drove Dot to bowling was concerned that Dot would wander off if she was left in the car while the friend ran an errand; therefore I drove Dot back and forth to bowling until the progression of the disease made it impossible for her to participate.

> **Tip**: *To prevent embarrassment limit social contact to people who understand the situation. When the patient can no longer participate positively in an organization it may be best to resign. However, socialize as long as possible which is beneficial for both the caregiver and patient.*
>
> **Tip**: *Do not leave an Alzheimer's patient unattended anywhere, they may wander away.*

The effects of the disease were becoming more apparent every day. At breakfast Dot would ask, "Are we going anywhere today?" She asked again and again though I had answered each time. She still understood short written sentences. I made a series of signs answering the frequent questions; like "We are not going anywhere today"; "We are going to the store", or "We are going to visit friends" and taped them to the sides of a lazy Susan. When she asked the question, I turned the lazy Susan and pointed to the answer. She then stopped asking repeatedly.

I also made a more comprehensive list of questions and answers for other people who attended her in my absence.

> **Tip**: *Prepare signs for the patient you can point to with answers to repeated questions.*
> **Tip**: *Compose for someone in attendance during your absence, a list of questions that the patient asks frequently and the answers.*

She asked, "Where are we?" I answered, "On the outskirts of Phillipsburg". If I had said "We lived in Allentown", she would not have accepted that answer. Likewise if I had said, "Your parents are in Phillipsburg and we live in our own house", she was satisfied.

The caregiver may be challenged consistently by the same question until a satisfactory answer that placates the patient is worded.

> **Tip**: *Give consistent answers that are acceptable to the patient, which probably may not be reality. Pacifying the patient is better than upsetting them.*

When Dot looked outdoors she said, "This is my parents' backyard"; she had spotted the bench we had retrieved from her father's yard in Phillipsburg years ago. Its presence firmly convinced her we were in her parents' home.

Cuttings from a neighbor's tree were scheduled to be removed in the spring, but Dot could not understand why her father left them there. She constantly complained, and I tried unsuccessfully to explain. Finally the neighbor and I moved them out of her sight.

> **Tip**: *Items from the past may trigger memories. Remove those that cause the patient to become disturbed or upset.*

Sun-downing behaviors

Continuous incoherent speech about unrelated subjects and semi-sentences I called a babble episode. Dot started talking in her sleep. I tried to nudge her awake, but got no response. A month later the length of time and intensity of babble conversation changed. One night I put her to bed around 10:00 pm; she slept a few hours and then babbled straight through until dawn. I discussed it with the doctor and he changed the medication schedule.

Tip: *When there is a vast change in sleeping habits, report it to the doctor for recommendation.*

Dot started to talk to herself, or to imaginary people. If I tried to interrupt, she did not acknowledge me. The babble was a conversation, usually criticism, denying something, or arguments with imaginary people. I learned from a friend that Dot used to have arguments with members of the ladies auxiliary; perhaps they were the imaginary people? The babbling occurred day or night and continued for one to two hours. Then she returned to normalcy with only a hint of Alzheimer's. At times her behavior with unseen people was a happy, laughing conversation at a party or gathering. She not only laughed with these people, but slowly reached her arms out as if to touch or hug them. I asked who they were. "Just them". I never got a name. Her mind-set seemed to be the years between high school and when she was employed at Ingersoll Rand.

She had discussions with room decorations, her image in a mirror or the imaginary person sitting next to her. I caught some sentences on various subjects, some I was unaware she knew anything about, like politics or current events in the world. Dot looked a lot like her mother. Peering into a mirror she saw her mother, and engaged in conversations or arguments with her mother for a half hour or more.

She did not recall any of the babble when she came out of the episode. Babbling only occurred once outside our house when I found her in the rain talking to a car.

A nurse who had worked in an Alzheimer's facility said this was typical "sun-downing". Why it occurs or how to stop it remains unknown. During the winter days it started around 4:00 p.m. and lasted about an hour. When winter waned, I thought if the sun set later in spring and summer, the daily sun-downing would occur later in the day. This did not happen; it still occurred at 4:00 pm, almost every evening. While sun-downing she had no problem navigating from room to room. If I was in the kitchen during an episode and it got too quiet, I immediately had to find her.

> **Tip**: *Do not try to interrupt a patient's conversation during sun-downing, you are locked out. You have to let it run its course.*

Looking back I remembered, after we were married for several years, we noticed that Dot's father, Willard, yelled at his wife Arvilla, and claimed that she was lazy, burnt the dinner or was just plain forgetful. She never said much unless she was with Dot or neighborhood housewives.

When my job responsibilities changed and we moved from our home in Bloomsbury, NJ to Allentown, PA, which was 25 miles from Dot's parents we noticed that the situation with Dot's parents seemed to deteriorate more each year. At the time we attributed it to their domestic status. Willard retired, but always complained about his wife's behavior. On one occasion Arvilla had a small heart attack that resulted in a heart by-pass operation. Her memory and attention span worsened, but no alert was taken.

When Dot's father suffered a fatal heart attack Dot's mother was at a complete loss. She did not want to stay in their home and sold it within months, and we moved her into an apartment. We went to visit Arvilla after the move and found her confused. We discovered also little pieces of paper throughout the apartment with notes on them, usually the same note. She couldn't remember where items were located in the apartment. We thought her confusion was due to the fact she had not been involved physically in the moving process, so we showed her where things were located. It seemed she could not retain the information. At times when we visited her she seemed okay, but would comment "I don't know what I'm doing."

We realized something was wrong, and spoke to her doctor who ordered a senior assessment. The doctor diagnosed Alzheimer's disease.

The family was unfamiliar with these diagnoses or its prognosis and she was moved into a small assistant living home. She finally settled down, but as time progressed, she began to look through her roommate's possessions and exhibited other unacceptable behaviors. After five more years she became violent to the point that management said it was necessary to move her into an Alzheimer's unit. When I visited, patients would ask if I was their son or husband. Many were in wheelchairs lined up like soldiers along the hallways. Others played children's games as a group, threw beach balls or sang songs. The facility was clean, but there was a light sour-sweet odor throughout the unit. It was very depressing.

Dot visited a few times, but her mother did not recognize her. Now and then Arvilla did recognize me. Eventually Dot waited outside while I visited. Dot said: "If I get Alzheimer's don't put me in a home like this." I promised I would not.

In hindsight, knowing what I do now, I'm sure Dot's mother had Alzheimer's in the early 60"s, but none of us knew anything about the disease. Consequently Willard scolded her without knowing that she was suffering the effects of Alzheimer's. Dot's mother died as a result of complications from pneumonia. She was 83 years old.

Patient Behaviors

Sometimes Dot addressed me as if I were the imaginary person with whom she was having a conversation. She repeated what the imaginary person said. I would answer, "If you cannot say something nice, don't say anything"; she replied "Well that is what the other person said". Normally Dot did not swear, but in the conversations with me there was some light swearing. I said "Don't swear" she replied "That is what the other person said".

> **Tip**: *Even though you are physically present, mentally the patient talks and answers you as if you were the invisible person or persons. Do not respond with an aggressive statement, it may make the situation worse.*

Medications wreak havoc with sleep patterns. The combination of medicines took its toll and most days she slept 10 to 12 hours a day. She woke up anytime between 10:00 am to 1:00 pm. I tried to coax her to stay up, but she insisted on going back to bed. While awake she resisted taking any pills. She spit them out. I called the doctor to find out if was alright to break up the pill, and then tried crushing it into yogurt or pudding

>**Tip**: *Take advantage of long sleep periods to accomplish chores or try to relax.*

Wedding album

Dot asked "Who are you?", "I am your husband", "No, I don't believe it". Conversation did not convince her. I resorted to our 45 year old wedding album that showed pictures of her getting ready for the wedding, the ceremony, the reception and leaving for the honeymoon. After awhile she was convinced that we were married and I was her husband, but the same scenario repeated itself numerous times. I felt downhearted when she didn't remember who I was, but it is another reality that the caregiver may experience.

>**Tip**: *Remember where you put that wedding album, I needed it quite often.*
>
>**Tip**: *Many times, the patient may not recognize you as you approach them from the front. Go behind them and speak to them. They may recognize your voice.*

Denial

When objects dropped and broke, or were moved, or drinks spilled or clothing was undone Dot denied doing any of it. This behavior accelerated as time went on, and her response to me always was "I did not do it". I learned not to say anything about an incident, even if I saw it. If I made any remark she became upset. She did not know reality, or mean to do anything wrong.

>**Tip**: *Pack away or remove breakable items. Learn to take these situations in stride and quietly take charge.*

Therapy

As a result of a fall Dot was prescribed therapy three times a week. Due to her resistance to getting out of bed, I made appointments as late as possible in the afternoon. I did not tell her where or when we were going to therapy. She asked "Why are we here?" as I opened the door to the therapy room. She was upbeat with the trainers and enjoyed the session. Her personality seemed to change back to her own self. The presence of others rejuvenated her. For assurance, I stayed next to her as she exercised. By the time we returned to the car her personality reverted back to forgetfulness. I tried to convince her to exercise at home without success. After three months, most of her motion was recovered.

> **Tip**: *Make appointments later in the day or at a time that causes less anxiety for the patient.*
>
> **Tip**: *Trying to coax a latter stage Alzheimer's patient to do exercise at home is frustrating.*

Medication Interaction

Another complication was that the pain medicine reacted negatively with the Alzheimer medication, and escalated sun-downing.

> **Tip**: *Be aware how medications may counter-interact. Some Alzheimer's medication escalates sun-downing.*

Falls

Dot was in the family room which was three steps lower than the kitchen. She tried to come upstairs, slipped and fell, and broke her left shoulder. It did not require a cast, but a sling. It was very difficult to explain to someone suffering from Alzheimer's for eight years to wear a sling in order for an injury to heal.

> **Tip**: *As a precaution to prevent falls, remove all throw rugs, and any objects that could cause tripping.*
>
> **Tip**: *Check footwear for non-slip soles.*

Dead-weight-lift

Another time Dot fell and landed on her back. Nothing seemed broken. I put my arms under her armpits to pull her up. No luck, I had 145 pounds of dead weight. She kept saying "I cannot get up." I rolled her onto her side, then onto her knees, and into a chair. Later I referred to First Aid books and the internet for "How to lift a person"; nothing.

The local Emergency Squad gave me the following information: Kneel behind the fallen person, put your arms under the armpits, and crisscross your arms in front of the victim. Grab their opposite wrists with your left hand on their right wrist then place your right hand on their left wrist. Using your legs, slowly stand up and hope the victim comes with you.

> **Tip**: *Go to your local emergency squad and learn how to lift up a person.*
> **Tip**: *If the patient uses a walker, make the pathway wide enough to allow for the width of the walker.*

Amusements

Sometimes I took her out to get an old fashioned ice cream soda, and we both reminisced about our early childhoods. She really enjoyed these outings.

Dot was excited that we are going for a glider ride to see the foliage. I was very apprehensive because Dot was afraid of roller coasters. I thought she might be frightened in the glider, but she had a wonderful time and said she would do it again. Likewise in September, a ski resort offered a ski-lift ride to the top of a mountain to view the foliage. To my surprise and delight she enjoyed the ride.

> **Tip**: *Even though the patient is in a latter stage of the disease, it does not mean they cannot enjoy an untried adventure. It is good for both parties, for me it was seeing her excitement as we flew like eagles.*
> **Tip**: *Take the patient out so they can relax and enjoy a change of scene.*

Travel

Dot realized she could not drive and decided to relinquish her license, which was much better than suggesting she should stop driving. For her to have an official identification while traveling, I obtained a Pennsylvania identification license. I made a copy and added the words "Alzheimer's Patient". Then I made a necklace for her to wear over her outer wear. She did not realize what it was or it's purpose; nor did she twiddle with it.

Tip: *When traveling the Alzheimer's patient needs to have obvious identification on outer wear.*

I belonged to a national industrial organization and once a year our spouses were invited to the annual event. I had insisted Dot travel to the meeting with the hope that once there she would enjoy seeing old friends. At the meetings the wives met for a pre-arranged tour, but Dot adamantly refused to leave her room to go along with them. When I questioned her about it, she said she just did not want to go. Yet, at that evening's dinner she appeared normal and engaged in conversation. I was confused by her behaviors. These mood swings were embarrassing and unpredictable for all concerned especially Dot and I.

Tip: *There will be a time when the patient realizes that their illness is noticeable to others and they withdraw.*

If I told Dot beforehand we were going to take a trip, or had a doctor's appointment, she would flatly refuse to get out of bed. After much pleading, I got her dressed; she even gave me a hard time getting into the car. When we arrived at our destination, she was very pleasant; all resistance was forgotten. This phase was becoming more prominent. I learned not to tell her when we had an appointment or a trip was planned.

Tip: *Do not inform future plans to the latter stage Alzheimer's patient to avoid resistance. Calmly lead them along and explain as you go.*

I planned for us to visit my sister in Florida and scheduled the latest flight, assuming Dot would be up in the afternoon, she refused to get up. I called Florida and placed the phone at Dot's ear knowing she would recognize my sister's voice. The conversation was enough to entice Dot to get up and to dress for the flight.

We visited my sister in Florida for a few weeks in March 2006. Initially Dot did not want to stay, but wanted to go home to Phillipsburg. I said "We are going on vacation" and that her parents (deceased) knew. It took a couple of days for her to settle at my sister's home. I left for a business trip for five days. On the third night my sister called. Dot told my sister, this was her house and my sister should get out. Needless to say, my sister was frightened. She was able to calm Dot, and I returned the next day. I had thought a visit with my sister would be enjoyable for Dot. That was our last trip.

> **Tip**: *Travel is not a good option in the late stages of Alzheimer's.*
> **Tip**: *It is amazing what someone else's voice can do when yours cannot. The patient may respond and cooperate with someone other than the caregiver.*

In the airport we tried an escalator. She did not want to step onto it, but with coaxing she finally did so. If I got on first, she could be left behind, if she went first and hesitated, I could crash into her. The solution was to step on together side by side and for me to guide her. Once on the escalator she was okay. Six months before she had no problems with escalators.

> **Tip**: *Take an elevator whenever possible. Last resort is stationary steps. However, the patient may tire very easily.*
> **Tip**: *Use the side-by-side technique on moving walkways.*

The Atlanta airport subway runs from terminal to terminal. We arrived at our terminal to find a car with open doors. I held Dot's hand, but let go briefly to hold the door open. Quickly she backed off and the doors started to close. She was on the platform, I was inside the car. She looked terrified. Another man helped me pry the doors open. I shudder to think what would have happened if she was separated and alone. Her only identification was the Alzheimer's card around her neck.

Tip: *Slow your pace to accommodate the patient. So what if you miss a connection when you travel? Allow sufficient time to avoid missteps.*

Traveling with an Alzheimer's patient is a difficult endeavor for the caregiver, the patient, and fellow travelers. I do not recommend it. Dot's attention span continued to diminish. She could not understand why we waited in line to go through inspection; much less remove jacket and shoes, and then the procedure reversed on the other side.

Tip: *Consider slip-on footwear, and omit any metal article.*

CHAPTER 2
Adjustments

Aricept was prescribed during the first eight and one half years. Namenda was added later in the hope of sustaining long-term and some short-term memory. The dosage and time of day medications were administered changed throughout that period. Degeneration slowed until the end of 2004, and increased the following year. Finally in October it really became noticeable. At that point it was decided the medicine was no longer effective, and was stopped for three weeks. No change in her mental well-being was noted. She was put back on the prescriptions for two weeks; again no change. By May I was pretty much on 24/7 duty. My saving grace was the times she slept 10 to 12 hours, allowing me the opportunity to accomplish chores and other tasks, like paying bills and shopping.

Tip: *Life for the caregiver changes, just doing simple activities can be trying.*

Appointments

My task was to make appointments for hairdresser, family doctor, OBGYN exam, dentist, eye doctor, and mammography. I was the one who was in anguish to learn the results of the mammogram and Pap tests. From October 2005 to May 2006 because of Dot's erratic waking time, fulfilling some of the appointments were hit and miss. I made the appointments for mid to late afternoon after she woke.

Assisted Living Homes

I visited five facilities all within a ten mile radius of our house. Three were for seniors some had dementia facilities; two had an additional wing for Alzheimer's. The rates in 2006 were $3400 to $4000 per month or $50,000 to $60,000 per year. This did not include telephone, TV, modem charges, cost of diapers, tissues, medicines or beauty parlor.

Tip: *When selecting a facility make sure it is Medicare certified so if you run out of funds or receive less than $2000 a month, Medicare may take over. If the home is not certified when the patient is admitted, they may face eviction when the pot runs dry. Get advice from a lawyer who is familiar with Elder Law issues because the government can change the rules. If one claims lack of funds, you must have given away or used up your assets five years prior to applying for assisted living. If you choose full day care or 24 hour care at home it can be much more expensive than assisted living. But remember, assisted living is usually staff limited for the needs of the patients.*

Geriatric Assessment

April 2005, Dot had lost the overall picture of life and daily activities. It was suggested, and I agreed, to have a group of geriatric specialists and social workers come to the house to review Dot's case. They asked Dot questions, but she could not understand their meaning. When they finished the studies; the diagnosis was the same as the family doctor's original diagnosis.

Tip: *Sometime a geriatric assessment is beneficial.*

Relief for the caregiver

By March 2006, my biggest concern was my mental health. Physically, except for weight lost, I stayed in good shape. However, sleep was continuously interrupted by Dot's babbling or waking in the middle of the night. I had to get things done before she woke in late morning. Once she was up I had to be alert at all times. I spoke to the doctor. He prescribed an anxiety pill that I took once or twice a day, depending on the situation. He also advised me to seek some relief help at home.

Tip: *When you feel exhausted mentally or physically do not hesitate to seek professional help.*

The caregiver, as the disease intensifies, experiences the loss of meaningful conversations. When you do have an opportunity to speak to others, you almost forget how. Fortunately I belonged to a national organization that I remained very active in, and corresponded and communicated via e-mail, teleconferencing and letters.

> **Tip**: *The caregiver needs to make a concerted effort to stay connected to the outside world.*

Assistance

End of March 2006, I kept a vigilant eye on Dot all the time. I felt as if I was living two lives. From exhaustion and lack of sleep I lost another five pounds in two months. I needed some relief. The Alzheimer's association advised me what was available for day care, assisted living and Alzheimer's facilities. At the time, the cost of the hour session of advice was $150. Day care can work in two ways; you may take the patient to them, or they can come to your home. If I took Dot to a day care, I found they have a schedule for activities from 8:00 am to 4:00 pm. The patient does not have to attend the entire eight hours, but you pay for the whole day. Since Dot slept late I could not get her to a day care until maybe 1:30 pm, so I dropped that option. I considered day care at home. Some agencies required a minimum of four hours. I chose not to use them. The rate was $25 to $30 per hour and more on weekends. I did locate an agency that did not have minimum hours, I employed them.

At this point Dot usually slept until noon. An assistant came Wednesdays from 12:00 pm to 2:00 pm. The woman bathed, dressed and prepared lunch for Dot. She mopped the kitchen floor, did light dusting and laundry. I used this time to grocery shop, or to pick up something at the mall or hardware store or bank. Unfortunately, on Wednesday afternoons there is not much entertainment to attend. I went to the town park for a walk and took advantage of the time to visit five assisted living homes.

> **Tip**: *Arrange for assistance in the middle of the week, or any suitable time in your schedule, to provide relief from the stress.*

Religious service

Church services became problematic because Dot's attention span had deteriorated, so I found a religious program on TV that she seemed to enjoy.

Tip: *Some type of religious service is beneficial for both parties.*

Holidays

As Alzheimer's progresses, the joy of the holidays slowly diminishes. Dot wanted to see the little goblins and give them candy at Halloween. By Thanksgiving she was quiet at the family gathering and I had to cut her food. She did not really understand the Christmas holidays anymore. I put up the tree, and had to remind her where her favorite ornaments were on the tree. We stayed home during Easter because I wished the extended family to remember Dot the way she used to be.

Tip: *The family may encourage the caregiver to decorate for the holidays, but are not always available to help. In reality as the disease progresses the caregiver needs to utilize time for other things, and may need to downsize the amount of decorations and holiday traditions.*

General information
Bed Linens

This is for those who are not familiar with bed, mattress and sheet sizes.

Sheets

I learned that sheets are available in a variety of sizes and thread count, the higher the number, the tighter the weaves per square and more costly. Various sheet materials are cotton, poly, linen or silk. The trial of putting a fitted bottom sheet on the mattress is a trial of patience.

Tip: *To help yourself, use a permanent marker to note "End" on both ends of a fitted sheet.*
Tip: *Metric size sheets will not fit on an American dimensioned mattress.*
Tip: *Make sure the bottom sheet is the right depth for the mattress.*

Mattress cover

Some mattress covers have a plastic protective cover to shield and keep the mattress dry. In the winter the plastic makes the bed warmer; but in the humid hot summer the plastic is very uncomfortable.

Tip: *Use a non-plastic mattress cover in the summer with a water-resistant pad.*

Cleaning the house

This is for the beginner and those who just don't like to do it:

I learned about layers of dust, mysterious dust webs and great gray balls of dust. Somewhere I read that a post-graduate wrote his doctoral thesis on dust formations. At first I laughed, in retrospect, it may be an interesting subject. When I first started, I could not believe how much dust formed overnight and gathered in strange places in big balls, especially in the closets, or how it makes a film on everything. I found a big vacuum cleaner was awkward to handle. I bought two small electric sweepers, one for upstairs, one for downstairs. They are much lighter with adjustable handles.

The places with the most germs in the house are refrigerator door and toilet handles.

Tip: *Have a box of handi-wipes convenient in the kitchen and bathrooms.*
Tip: *A small light weight electric sweeper is easier and quicker to use, especially when time is precious.*
Tip: *I use a dust mop whose handle extends to twelve feet to clean cobwebs in the stairwells and hallway.*

The Garden

I'm a gardener, and March is the time to clear the gardens of winter debris. If Dot slept late, I kept the motion detector receiver in my pocket while gardening. It activated 50 feet from the detector.

Dot liked to sit in the sun near me. In early spring the soil thaws, and her chair's legs sank into the soft lawn. I had to switch to chairs with wider feet, and placed a piece of rug under her feet to keep warm. Sometimes she walked around picking up sticks, or discovered merging flowers or pointed out the shape of clouds. I went to her so she could show me what was giving her joy. She liked to share her discovery.

In the garden I hooked the fence gates closed, and was continuously alert to where she was. I did not want her to wander to the street or go back into the house.

Locking the house doors backfired on me one day. I had hooked the front door closed, and took Dot outside so I could garden. Before I knew it, she felt chilly, went inside, and locked the back door. I knocked on the back door; she could not turn the knob to unlock the door. I did not have a copy of the key with me. Dot cried inside the house. I climbed on the roof to an open window, got in, found Dot and calmed her.

> **Tip**: *Have extra keys made to hide outside and give one to a neighbor. Or leave a window on the first level unlocked. Remember to lock it when you leave the house.*
>
> **Tip**: *When you are outdoors and may become distracted, pin a bell on the patient.*

Walking

Dot liked to walk outside. The sidewalk next to the house had a slightly raised gutter for run-off. As she rounded the corner, I said, "Be careful of the run-off."; however, she misjudged the distance between the corner and walkway and fell. She was not hurt. It took awhile to calm her and to get her to stand. I placed a 6 foot tall trellis at the run-off between the sidewalk and house. This guided her around the corner onto the walk.

Tip: *As the disease progresses, patients lose their sense of balance. Make sure they have something to grip to prevent falls. A caretaker should always be present.*

Tip: *Make wide pathways to walk on in a garden.*

She liked to take about a 20 minute walk in the late afternoon in the winter or summer evenings. It was important that walks corresponded to bodily functions.

I learned before the walk to make sure she had a handkerchief(s), and I had extras. This was especially needed during pollen season. In the latter stage of the disease I made sure shoe laces were tied, coat, sweater or blouse were buttoned or zipped. In the winter made sure she had gloves, hat and scarf. I removed laces from hoods and jackets to prevent her from fidgeting continuously.

Tip: *It is important for the patient and caregiver to exercise and socialize. Go to a park or walk around a Mall. Many have early senior walk-a-thorns before business.*

Tip: *Remove loose laces from hoods and jackets.*

Laundry

Learning to manage the clothes washer was a steep learning curve, water temperatures, load size, type of clothes; normal, casual, permanent press, delicate or hand washable, spin or no spin. The major problem was remembering to take the laundry out of the hamper. Different types of soaps; fragrance or none, soften or not, to bleach or not, for colors or not, I ended up using "warm water and load size".

Had to remember when the washing machine buzzed finish to put the clothes in the drier so wrinkles did not set. The clothes dryer was almost as bad; automatic dry, timed dry or fluffed air, the temperature choices of extra-low, low, medium or heavy, depending on the size of the load. To keep wrinkles to a minimum I was advised to hang articles as soon as the dryer stopped. Ironing was a hurdle. A "How to do" book illustrated how to iron shirts, blouses and pants. I sent the better garments to the cleaners. Purchased long flat plastic zippered boxes designed to go under a bed. This worked great to store bed linens. I gained bureau space and knew where the linens were.

Clothing

Dot put her hands in the pockets of her garments when walking. I reminded her over and over to take her hands out of the pockets. I worried if she fell with her hands in the pockets; she would not have time to pull her hands out to block a fall.

In the winter gloves made it awkward to put her hands into the pockets, but she kept taking them off, so I attached double backed Velcro in the pocket opening, but that was unsatisfactory. Then I sewed the pockets shut. I found that she did not miss the pockets.

Dot's slacks could not have a belt, because she fiddled with the buckle, but needed side pockets. This had pros and cons. The pockets were good so she had a place for a handkerchief, bad because she put her hands in the pockets. During the last six months I sewed the pockets shut.

Her winter jacket had two pull laces to make the jacket snug, one around the neck and the other below the waist. I would get her all bundled up with laces tight but after we had walked a short distance she would take off her gloves and readjust the laces. It did not matter if I said anything, this would continue as we walked.

> **Tip**: *Pull out laces- they won't be missed, better to buy clothing with Velcro closures.*
> **Tips**: *Sew pockets shut; or purchase clothing without pockets.*
> **Tip**: *In the latter stages of the disease blouses or tops should be plain without ruffles or embroidery, or zippers to fiddle with. Some patients may not have the arm coordination to wear a garment that fits over the head.*

I noticed Dot's bra straps kept slipping off her shoulders; she was forever reaching under her blouse to pull them up. I tried adjusting the strap length to no avail.

Tip: *I bought two eight inch long by one inch wide Velcro straps. One end had a slot to pass the other end through. I looped them around the bra straps pulling them closed and secured them in place. Now the bra straps stayed in place.*

I smiled at times while putting the bra on Dot; she asked "What are these straps for?" I said "to support your breasts". Reply "Oh yes, that's right".

Tip: *I found that bras that hook in the front were easier for her to manage.*

For each season there were just so many clothes I wanted to circulate. I chose enough selections so she was not wearing the same thing week after week. I mixed and matched the colors. Some days, blues or black, other days she liked white and beige. I offered two or three selections, no more, because it became confusing for Dot. Sometimes she would say "No" to something. I would put it back and bring it out a minute later and it was okay.

Tip: *When a patient does not like the clothes selection, put it back, wait a minute and offer it again, it may be acceptable.*

Dot dressed herself until the end of summer 2005. With fall approaching it was time to start switching from summer to fall clothes. As she tried on fall clothes I noticed a lot of slacks were longer, by as much as an inch. I took them to my tailor. The doctor said the height loss was due to osteoporosis. He gave us sample medicine to try to slow it down. Like some other medications, it did not agree with the Alzheimer's medication. It upset her stomach so we just stopped it.

Tip: *Now and then try on seasonal clothes to determine if the body is changing.*

For Dot it was very important to always have a handkerchief. I ordered a dozen or more from the Vermont Country Store. I kept extras in the car so when we got half-way down the road I did not have to go back to get one.

Tip: *Keep extras handkerchiefs or Kleenex in the car, or on your person.*

Now and then Dot took off one shoe and sock and walked around with one shoe on, and one off. I don't know why. At times she would just take the laces out of her shoes. I did not enjoy this behavior and was concerned the loose shoe would cause her to fall. Also it was time consuming to re-lace her shoes. It was difficult for Dot to put on her own shoes, and I found a shoe horn made it much easier to slip her feet into her shoes.

> **Tip**: *Place the shoe horn upright between the heel and back of the shoe. Instruct the patient to push their foot into the shoe, at the same time the caregiver should slip the shoehorn under the heel of the foot and apply a gentle upward pressure to the heel of the shoe. Most shoe or department stores do not use shoehorns anymore. I obtained them at L. L. Bean.*
>
> **Tip**: *Buy sneakers or shoes with Velcro fasteners.*
>
> **Tip**: *A simple knot at the end of each shoelace prevents un-lacing.*

I took Dot to a women's shop and let them determine the size panties she wore. Once I knew the size I re-ordered them from a woman's clothing catalog. At first it was awkward until I established a rapport with the saleswomen.

> **Tip**: *After determining the patients garment sizes re-order over the phone.*

If a blouse, sweater or jacket had a zipper it meant trouble for me. First, she could not get them started, I had to do that. Once they were zipped up, she pulled the zipper up and down continuously.

> **Tip**: *I resorted to pinning a nice broach through the material and zipper latch. She liked the broaches and stopped playing with the zippers.*

Hygiene

Hygiene for an Alzheimer's patient is something a caregiver has to address. You may have never thought about doing this for someone else, but it is part of the journey and almost like caring for a baby. You must supervise a healthy diet and make sure there are no elimination problems. I hope these tips are beneficial.

As caregiver, I maintained Dot's finger and toe nails, made sure she brushed her teeth (with toothpaste), removed unwanted hairs, cleaned eyes, cleaned her glasses, combed her hair and every once in awhile she liked to put on lipstick. When she missed; I tried and messed it up again. So we laughed and tried one more time.

Eyes

In 2004 she could read simple sentences slowly. Even though she did not comprehend it; she liked going through the morning paper. I thought she might need new glasses. I tested her eyesight by asking if she saw different objects; it did not appear to be a problem. She pointed out small objects that she observed; this is quite different from referring to an object by the wrong name or color.

Tip: *Make an appointment annually for an eye examination.*

Hair

For years, Dot went to the same beauty parlor. When she no longer drove, I took her. This weekly trip continued until she was immobile. It was good for her and gave me an hour's break.

Tip: *Trips to the hairdresser or barber may provide a pleasurable experience for the patient and break for caregivers.*

Teeth

By year eight, I had to remind Dot to brush her teeth and had to assist her. I kept my brush at a separate location so she would not use it. As trying as this process was, at all semi-annual dental exams the dentist gave a good report.

Tip: *Daily dental care results in fewer problems.*

Nails

The caregiver has to maintain the patient's toes and toenails. Since she walked less and less it was important to keep her feet clean and dry, and the toenails clipped straight across.

> **Tip**: *I found white socks were easiest to maintain (they eliminated choices), and they helped to control any fungus infection.*

Dot used to spend a lot of time taking care of her nails. That stopped as the disease progressed, and I took over cutting and filing, but did not apply fingernail polish because she chewed it. Keeping her nails clean was a problem during the last months. She fiddled with the soil in the house plants consequently her fingernails required my constant care.

> **Tip**: *Remove or place plants where the patient cannot play with the soil.*

Toilet

As the disease progresses the patient has a harder time maneuvering to sit on the toilet. A toilet stand or a seat that straddles allows the patient to guide themselves to the seat.

> **Tip**: *When the time comes, buy a toilet stand that straddles the toilet. The patient may accidentally drop something down the toilet. Usually it can be retrieved with a plumber's snake.*
> **Tip**: *Try a non- rusting plumber's snake first before calling a repair man.*

Food and Meals

Groceries

Early on when I did the grocery shopping, Dot could still help. It allowed her to get out of the house to see people and things in the store. We patronized three supermarkets. One had better prices, but was a travel nightmare, I cancelled it out. The second was too crowded to watch Dot and shop at the same time. The third was calmer, which is important. The clerks and managers got to know us which helped. The in-house pharmacy was a boon; it meant one less store to shop. I dropped off the prescription as I entered the store; did the grocery shopping then picked up the prescription before I left the store.

Tip: *Grapefruit can interact negatively with some medication.*
Tip: *Establish a relationship with store personnel so the patient is not embarrassed.*

Setting the table

In the first eight years Dot would set the table in a normal manner, but then I noticed that the knife, fork and spoon were often misplaced or there would be two forks at one setting. I would quietly transfer them, and she would say "That's right". Then in October 2005 she started to misuse the knife for the fork, so I just gave her a spoon and fork. Since her portion was getting smaller, I put her meal on a smaller plate so she did not think she was getting shortchanged. From March 2005, now and then, she lost her coordination at the table and food fell from the table or her glass would spill. I changed the glass to a small paper cup. I bought a long bib that covered her knees. It opened around the neck with a Velcro attachment by the left shoulder. It worked better than an apron because it did not have to go over the head or tie around the waist.

She liked placemats on the table. However, I had to use ones with a plain surface. If it had a design or a picture, she would move the dinner plate aside to talk about the design. She always cleaned the mats. The time I put down mats of clear plastic was a bad move because she cleaned both sides continuously. This became an endless task so I put them away.

Tip: *Use unbreakable wares.*

Flatware

Our flatware was a setting for eight. However, I noticed that only six or seven pieces in the different dividers in the silverware drawer. I dug through the garbage and found the missing pieces, so I reduced the set of eight to four, that way I could easily count what was there. I did the same for cups, plates and glasses. Why not settle for two place settings? Because now and then we had company, and also I did not want the continuous wear on the set of two. Also when I used the dishwasher a set for two was still in the drawer.

Tip: *Downsize as much as possible.*

Meals

Unfortunately, Alzheimer's patients must take lots of pills, usually at breakfast, lunch and dinner and bedtime. I divided them in groups for each meal, that way I knew which pills I had given her during the day.

Maintaining a healthy diet is vital for a patient. They may revert to wanting sweets, or refuse to eat the healthy foods they liked formerly. The caregiver has to offer foods that appeal and is nutritious.

The first seven years Dot ate regular adult portions. Then her appetite waned. At times she ate three quarters of the serving. To compensate for change I gave her snacks of small hamburgers, puddings, fruit flavored yogurts, oatmeal-raisin cookies, energy bars, nuts or dried fruit.

We drank regular tea three times a day, but it did not agree with some medications. I switched to orange juice and milk in the morning, fruit juice or water at lunch, fruit juice, de-caffeinated tea or water for dinner. We shared a bottle of de-caffeinated soda once a day.

Except for the last two months, her weight varied plus or minus five pounds. Then there was a gradual loss of weight. I gave her smaller portions, so she could say she cleaned her plate. Lunch in the last three years was usually half a sandwich, she could not eat more. To get out of the house, now and then we went to a fast food establishment.

Tip: *Adjust meals to make sure the Alzheimer's patient eats a healthy diet. Establish a schedule for meals.*

Preparing the meals

In the last six months preparing a hot dinner and observing Dot was a challenge. If I sat her at the table, she kept moving the flatware and dishes. If I left her in the living room, I did not know what to expect. Meanwhile the pots were cooking. I did not serve too many frozen dinners. The microwave was a big help.

Tip: *Keep dinner simple but nutritious and attractive.*
Tip: *Take a break before dinner together. Use a timer to keep track of cooking times.*
Tip: *Guide the patient to the table.*
Tip: *A TV in the kitchen helps occupy the patient.*
Tip: *Use a long bib to protect clothing.*

Eating

Year seven, Dot had a hard time using utensils. She picked up a fork to put food into her mouth, but forgot to cut the food. From then on I cut it for her before serving. I no longer gave her a knife. To give me a break from cooking, we still went to restaurants, I asked for a booth or corner. I needed to cut her food and put it on the fork, she savored a bite of steak or salmon with a smile.

Tip: *The disease may cause the patient to have difficulty using utensils. Eventually you may have to feed the patient.*

Chores

She wanted to clean the dishes with the hot water, but not remembering how to use the soap, I said "I will wash and you can dry." This was okay with her. The problem was dropped plates. I switched to hard plastic plates. She did not understand that the ones on my right were not washed, but just rinsed off. She always picked that pile to dry. "I will let you know when to dry". Some dishes got dried two or three times, that was okay.

She did not know where to put the dishes away. I said "Just pile similar things", and then opened a cabinet door and showed her where to place them. We repeated the ritual for the silverware.

Tip: *Let the patient help as long as it is safe and enjoyable. Switch to washable plastic tableware.*

Chapter 3
Progression of the Disease

In the late 90's Dot took up needle point when she was in the beginning stages of Alzheimer's. These were complicated pictures requiring 30 different colored threads. She did one a year until 2003 when she experienced problems selecting the correct colors and threading the needle. The needlepoint was set aside. We tried jig saw puzzles next. That activity lasted for six months. She did okay during the winter of 2004; by winter 2005 her attention span had faded. February 2006 she could not follow most TV shows but seemed to enjoy Family Affair in the afternoon, and Jeopardy and Wheel of Fortune in the evening.

In March 2005 I tried playing CD music to interest Dot. She sang along with 1950's and 60's tunes but soon lost interest. I played a jazz station; she hummed the theme song whenever it aired. April I gave her children's books with lots of pictures. She had two favorites she carried around the house. By May she lost interest and carried small pieces of paper and envelopes (similar to what her mother did). I offered her a pen and pencil, but that was too much. She would tell me what was written on the blank paper and she was very firm about what it said. In lieu of a security blanket she carried a small pillow from room to room. After 8:00 pm she was in her own world. In two and a half years the aggressiveness of the disease affected her mental capacity If I talked to someone on the phone who knew Dot, I asked if she wanted to say hello; most of the time she said "No". I said "Come on". Reluctantly she took the phone and said a happy "Hello". Now and then the conversation went a little off-track; in general it sounded fine and was good for her to speak to someone other than me. To break up the 'just the two of us' routine, I asked her friends to call on the phone and have a small conversation with Dot. They did, and it made Dot happy.

Some afternoons or evenings we chatted with the neighbors. This was relaxing for me as well as for Dot. Now and then she would join in the conversation, but mostly listened, and she always said it was nice.

Tip: *For mental exercise, have the patient try jig saw puzzles.*
Tip: *Play CD's or radio stations that play music they enjoy.*
Tip: *Give them children's books with lot of pictures.*
Tip: *Substitute a small pillow instead of a security blanket for them to carry.*
Tip: *Outside communication is stimulating for the patient and provides a breather for the caregiver.*

To go downstairs, she held my one hand and the rail with her other hand. I held on to her and stepped backwards. The rail stopped before the last step, and she was concerned about falling off the last step. She kept reaching for a rail that was not there. I realized she was trying to tell me she needed something to hold. To get to the last step I took both her hands to guide her down the last step. Later I filled the void with railing. She could climb upstairs slowly by herself. I stayed behind her to make sure she didn't fall. I did observe when the babbling-wandering episodes occurred she could navigate both ways without a problem!

Her desire to go home to her parent's house in Phillipsburg grew stronger and stronger, so did her desire to leave our house. When wandering under an episode she went into the spare rooms or down the cellar stairs. I installed locking devices high on the doors.

She said "My parent's house is just around the corner." She unlocked and tried to open the front door held by the latch. She pulled the door handle back and forth countless times. If I tried to get her away from the door she became aggressive. Finally she stopped to have a conversation with someone unseen or snapped out of the episode.

Tip: *Secure doors to limit the patient's wandering.*
Tip: *Determine the door's internal construction before attaching latches. Some internal doors only have a one inch wide board frame under thin plywood or plastic.*
Tip: *I installed a latch high on the door frame where she could not reach, to keep the door locked securely.*

House plants

There were many plants in the front bay window, Dot liked to sit on the sill to look outside. I found green leaves in her hands and mouth, the plants were promptly moved.

Frustration

In February she began to grab the railings that were bolted to the wall and give them an awful pull, as if trying to tear them off. After two pulls she usually stopped. She pulled down wall shelves that were screwed to the wall and almost took a heavy mirror off the wall. I checked the bolts to make sure they were secure.

We had a wooden statue of a butler three feet high holding a tray. Dot went up to the butler and pulled the bolted tray right out of his hands, I left the tray off. I did not scold or reprimand her because if I did, she would say "I did not do that". I just guided her away. I left the butler there because she talked extensively to him.

Tip: Remove or check that all decorations and rails are securely attached. Remove all breakable objects.

Motion detectors

For safety, I needed to know when Dot was up during the night. As a result I was losing sleep while trying to keep alert. To get a handle on the situation, I bought a baby monitor. It worked pretty well, but did not always catch when she got up. Then I used a driveway motion detector. The mobile receiver picked up a signal from a distance of fifty feet, even from outdoors. Its sensitivity range even picked up her arm motion as she rolled over in bed. My sleep was undisturbed until the signal went off.

Tip: Purchase a motion detector to monitor the patient's movement in their bedroom.
Tip: Obtain a motion night light, that goes on with the slightest movement; it is brighter than a standard night light. It stays lit as

long as there is motion in the area, it goes off one minute after motion has ceased. It solved the problem of no lights on at bedtime.

Bedcovers

For years we had a blanket with a patchwork design. In the latter stages, Dot sat on the bed and toyed with the patchwork for long periods and refused to get in bed and go to sleep. This behavior was similar to her fixation with the placemats in the kitchen. When I changed the patchwork to a plain colored blanket the problem was solved.

Tip: *Use plain colored bedcovers and blankets.*

Rejection

When I heard Dot get up, I knocked on the bedroom door. She would not let me in, but I opened the door anyway, she shouted at me to get out. She became so aggressive I closed the door and left her. In minutes I heard her moving things. I did not know what I would find later. I worried if she was doing something destructive in the bathroom, or with the clothing, jewelry or bedding. Fortunately, I did not hear the toilet flush. When I slowly opened the door I found she had calmed down and was talking to and twiddling with the bedspread. She also had been investigating her jewelry box. The next day I moved her jewelry and perfume. Rejection behavior towards me occurred at least once a week or more.

Tip: *Aggressive behavior will usually calm down if the patient is ignored for awhile.*
Tip: *Remove any items that could be damaged or cause a problem, especially in the bathroom.*

Role change

Dot kept looking and asking for "Dad", I thought she was looking for her father. Then one day my sister realized that I was the "Dad" that Dot referred to. My role and identity had changed.

Tip: *Answer the patient according to the perceived identity.*

Affection

This disease depresses your spirit and the patient's as contact with reality and the outside world becomes more limited

Tip: *Give them a kiss and a hug at least once day to keep spirits uplifted.*

CHAPTER 4
Medication

This chapter chronicles nine years of prescribed medications to alter the progression of the disease and the side-effects encountered. Administering the various medications is a frustrating experience for the caregiver.

1997

Dot's Alzheimer's disease is diagnosed.

1998

Medication prescribed: Lipitor for high Cholesterol, Aricept for Alzheimer's and vitamin E for blood thinner. These medications and times to administer remained the same until 2002.

2002

The doctor switched Pepcid to Prilosec to soothe Dot's hiatal hernia because Pepcid upset her stomach in the morning.

2003

January- Sometimes after she woke Dot experienced leg cramps while in bed.

Tip: *Tonic water with quinine stopped the cramps for Dot.*

March – I noted Dot walked slower and her dementia seemed worse.

April - I sensed something else was wrong. Tests showed Dot's hemoglobin count to be 1.5, the normal range is 12.0. The doctor ordered two units of blood be administered. Dot did not comprehend why she was in the hospital and wanted to go home. She could not understand the nurse's questions, I answered them. After two days in the hospital her blood count was 8.8. The doctor prescribed iron pills three times a day, liver, spinach and anything else fresh that contained iron, which is much better to ingest than taking pills.

> **Tip**: *If there is a dramatic physical change in mobility consult the doctor immediately.*
> **Tip**: *Remember when a dementia patient is admitted to a hospital they are confused and cannot answer questions properly. The caregiver or other guardian must be present to answer questions.*

May - She was prescribed Hydrochlorot (HCL) for high blood pressure.

September - OBGYN exam confirms a bladder infection. Medication was prescribed. There was an interaction between the dementia and infection medicines resulting in an increase of Dot's repetitious stories. After the infection cleared, and the medication stopped, the repetitious cycle diminished considerably.

> **Tip**: *Beware of interaction of medicines.*

2004

Namenda was added to the prescribed Aricept to slow the dementia.

HCL tablets to lower blood pressure were increased to two tablets daily.

2005

I suspected that the bladder infection had returned. The doctor ordered Dot to drink lots of fluids to flush out the infection. Instead of drinking all fluids, a nurse suggested giving her popsicles. Dot really liked them and it was easier for all concerned.

> **Tip**: *If the patient is required to drink lots of fluids, popsicles are helpful.*

September – The doctor diagnosed that Dot had osteoporosis and prescribed a new medicine. She was sick for the next two days after taking the new medicine. The doctor said to stop the medication.

Tip: *Before giving a new medicine on a regular basis, be alert for side effects.*

We could not pinpoint why Dot did not feel well or slept late. The prescribed Hydrochlorot, Aricept, Lipitor and Namenda were continued. During the next few days I gave her the pills and she slept for long periods. When awake she was disoriented and not feeling well. Lexapro was used for anxiety. With Lexapro she slept 19 hours. The next morning she had a good day, but that night her shoulders, back and legs twitched for hours.

Tip: *Keep a log so the doctor may review what medications were given and when given.*

During 2005, many different medicines were prescribed, as well as changes in dosages, time of administration and types of chasers. For all of these attempts, the progress of Alzheimer's still marched on eluding positive results and frustrating me.

Tip: *Again I am stressing the importance for the caregiver to keep good records for the doctor to analyze which medications are the most effective and if there is any counter-indications noted.*

2006

Medications prescribed by the doctor:
1. HCT– for blood pressure, Mon-Wed-Fri in a.m.
2. Aricept - for Alzheimer's
3. Namenda - for Alzheimer's
4. Lipitor – for cholesterol, stopped for two weeks, then resumed
5. Lexapro – for depression, every other day
6. Ambien – for sleep
7. Amoxil –for bladder infection

I gave her an anxiety pill, it was not effective. She was awake all night and talked to me incoherently. She saw people in the bedroom; heard children in a garden, and wanted to know when we were leaving this place; kept thinking that there were other people in the house and wanted me to make sure we had groceries for a party. This was a totally new behavior. Finally she went to sleep at 5:30 am. This was completely different from 2005 when she slept continuously. The doctor recommended an additional Ambien a half hour after the first one if it was not effective.

> **Tip**: *Be prepared for extensive times that the patient is incoherent and exhibits new disturbing behaviors.*

At times the Alzheimer's or anxiety medicines would result in nausea, I found a glass of water or tablespoon of Pepto-Bismol relieved the nausea.

> **Tip**: *Sometimes it takes a simple thing like water, or over-the-counter remedies like Pepto-Bismol or Tums to settle the stomach.*

I observed that as the disease progressed, medication for Dot's ailments inter-acted negatively and caused various side-effects. She became nauseous, seemed to lose her balance, and became more disoriented. We changed dosages; times administered; combinations of medications; eliminated some. The doctor told me that eventually some medications would no longer be effective and stopped the Alzheimer's prescriptions. When this happened, she got up on her own and came downstairs in a good mood. She felt well during the day with only a little sun-downing in the evening. She went to bed on her own at 10:30 pm. I thought we had the right combination.

Joy was short lived. The next day she got up on her own, and after her morning routine she felt okay. She had light sun-downing most of the day, accepted that her parents and sister were in heaven; in the evening she hallucinated. She told me the phone rang, and it was for her father. She told me that there were people in the house and wanted me to drive her home. This behavior continued for a week. I had traded good days for worse sun-downing and hallucinations than before.

The doctor made an appointment for a brain MRI: one had been done seven years previously. The results showed no change in the MRI, but her mental well-being had deteriorated radically!

The dementia medication was not effective and Dot slept 11 to 14 hours a day. The sun-downing and hallucinations were worse than ever. The doctor prescribed a combination of drugs to combat some of these problems. We switched times and dosages of medication frequently trying to find the best format for Dot. Meanwhile Dot's moods swung from aggressive in the morning, silly in the afternoon, to sun-downing at night.

The doctor prescribed a different anti-depressant which was supposed to take effect two weeks later, but it produced a living hell almost immediately. Dot became more depressed and very aggressive. Her mind produced major hallucinations that lasted for an hour or more. The cycle of babbling, sun-downing, hallucinations, aggressiveness and sleeping intensified. I suspected it was the new drug that had been introduced to reduce the anxiety. In desperation I changed the time I gave her the new anxiety pill. That seemed to do the trick, Dot felt better for the next couple of days. Unfortunately, Dot fell soon afterwards and her erratic behaviors accelerated.

CHAPTER 5
Going Home

Mother's Day 2006, we were having our evening snacks when Dot looked out the window and said, "I want to go home". She turned and instead of going around the end of the table she walked toward the middle of the table. "Dot, go around the end". It was too late, she just kept walking forward. Then as if in slow motion, she started to fall over the table, then slid sideways landing on her right leg. At the same time her shoulder, then her head, hit a room divider, it swayed back and forth as knick-knacks rained down. A glass bowl with serrated edges just missed Dot's head. She lay there crying. I cradled her head, she cried and cried. There was no blood, just coconut-pineapple drink all over her face and hair. I could not get her up she just kept on crying. I called my neighbor Tim. We lifted her onto the couch. She calmed down somewhat, but as soon as I touched, or asked her to move her leg, she cried. When Dot fell my immediate reaction was she had broken a leg or hip. I fearfully pictured a cast, pain pills, and all kinds of reactions to those pills. The emergency squad arrived and took her to the Emergency Room. Thank goodness X-rays showed nothing was broken, she had a bad bruise. It was a traumatic experience for Dot. I took her home. The next afternoon incontinence became apparent, and Dot did not communicate with my neighbor Gail or me. I started to think that this was more than just a reaction to the fall. Dot became incoherent. I called the doctor's office to ask him to come to the house. They responded, "The doctor does not make house calls". If I brought Dot there they would meet us with a wheelchair. I said, "I could not do that." The doctor called to say he ordered Hospice Care to come to the house. The realization of what was happening descended on me like a weight. Now it was a question of when.

Hospice

I became aware of a wonderful organization, Hospice, in the last days of my mother's life. Their charter is to help people return to health, but in most cases the care is for the terminally ill. Hospice is not a national organization like the Red Cross. They are independent organizations, usually associated with a church or hospital. I have heard only high praise from those families who experienced Hospice care for loved ones. These are special people providing nursing care and a chaplain to support the family. They make you and the patient feel comforted by forming a bond with the family during end days.

Hospice arrived within two hours of engagement; they set up a motorized hospital bed in the living room and positioned it so Dot could look out the bay window. They brought all the supplies even a wheelchair and walker, but most of all wonderful, caring people. The installers departed after the equipment was set up, but Dot was still upstairs. Tim, Gail's husband, and I used the holding method I learned from the Emergency Squad to carry Dot down to the hospital bed.

A packet of medication arrived the next day by FedEx. The packet information explained each medicine, and when and how to administer them. Some medicines were for immediate use and others for future use. The nurse explained all the medicines to me. Some were sealed, and some had to be refrigerated. When a doctor calls for Hospice the major portion of the billing goes to Medicare.

Nightgown

Tip: *Dot's long nightgowns were cut up the back from the bottom to almost the neckline transferring them into hospital gowns.*

Diapers

Tip: *Diapers were necessary and the nurse instructed me how to use them. I was instructed to give Dot a pill to calm her 20 minutes before a change.*

I moved the motion detector downstairs aimed at her bed. I was awakened at 2:00 am to find Dot lying in bed reaching out to the imaginary people in front of her. She was laughing with them, and unaware that I was there. I raised the position of the detector and went back to bed. Most of the day, she lay with her eyes closed, hardly spoke, much of the time she was asleep.

Mirror

> **Tip**: *I braced a big mirror on the living room floor at an angle so I could see her in bed from the kitchen. Now and then Dot lightly waved to me and visa versa.*

The Hospice aides arrived in the morning to change, wash, put on lotion, comb her hair and brush her teeth. Dot smiled when her hair was combed. A week after the fall Dot still cried when we changed her position in the bed. We suspected a hairline crack in her hip that was not picked up by x-rays.

The nurse visited every other day. If a change in medicine was needed, she called the doctor. It was delivered the next morning by FedEx. Dot kept taking off the sheets and blanket. Her metabolism had completely reversed from before her fall and she now felt too warm.

Food

The nurse said to feed her baby food, Ensure, athletic liquid, or nectar, but no water. Water was too thin and could easily go down the wrong throat passage leading to pneumonia.

> **Tip**: *Keep the patient's head and back raised to insure the liquid d flows in the right direction, too much liquid at a time resulted in coughing.*

Gail brought me baby food. The labels said "Remove the top and microwave for 30 seconds", let it cool before serving. I went to the store to get more baby food; it had been over 36 years since I last bought baby food. Things had changed. The food is shelved by Numbers 1 to 4. The food viscosity increases as the number on the label gets higher. My nephew who was with me, called his wife for help. She advised me to buy Number 2 jars.

I assumed the new jars used the same heating instruction as the ones Gail gave me. I opened a jar, placed it in microwave for 30 seconds. As I turned around there was an explosion behind me. I turned to see orange food splashed all over inside the microwave. What caused this? I wiped the jar; on the side was a small yellow label "Do not microwave it may splatter". Forget the "may" it should say "it will" splatter. I called the manufacturer's customer service and suggested they put the warning label on the top of the lid and in bigger, bolder letters. What a mess to clean up!

>   **Tip**: *Don't assume the heating instructions are the same from one jar of food to the next. Read the labels.*

Calories

Throughout the day I fed Dot baby food, nectars, Ensure and laxative. Even though she was not eating much; it was important to have a bowel movement. Total calorie consumption for the day was 600, the nurse was hoping for 1200.

Counting calories can be a challenge. The amount of calories per serving was on the label, but what, "was a serving"; it changed from product to product. It was challenging to divide, multiply and add up the calories for different foods. I bought a package that had two containers of pears. The label said 35 calories. Was it calories per container or a total for the two servings? I called the manufacturer's customer service, they did not know for sure, but assumed it meant 35 per container. May 25, total calories are down to 200.

>   **Tip**: *You may have to call the food manufacturer to determine the calories per serving.*

The nurse was concerned about bed sores. She brought two, three inches thick, foam mattresses to the house. One mattress was placed under the sheet that Dot lay on. The nurse asked me to cut the other mattress lengthwise and to put the halves on the floor on each side of the bed. This was a precaution if Dot tried to get out of bed or fell out of the bed; she would land on the foam rather than the hardwood floor. The events of the week had not allowed time to schedule an aide or nurse for the weekend. My neighbors had prior engagements, I was on my own. Hospice gave me an emergency phone number, which I used. The weekend was nerve racking, but we survived. This all took a toll on me.

Her intake was 200 calories. I swabbed her mouth with wet Q-tips to keep it moist. The next day the intake was zero. Morphine was administered by droplets under the tongue. The nurse told us Dot had about 72 hours. She told me that the brain was shutting down.

Tip: *I was told to keep her feet raised and separated to assure circulation and prevent rubbing sores.*

June second Dot passed away. "Dot, Yoo-Hoo, you got your Mother's Day wish, you are home now," Don't let the bed bugs bite."

It was a powerful experience to be able to keep Dot home until she died. It enabled me to give her constant loving care. I felt drained and empty when she was gone.

Funeral arrangements

With the realization of the inevitable, I had called a funeral home to make arrangements. They came to the house to discuss the arrangements. They advised me to contact our church to make arrangements also.

Funeral Home

Some time before Dot died I had contacted the Church and funeral home to make arrangements for cremation as we had decided.

After she died, I collected myself and I called Hospice who notified the undertaker. They arrived immediately and took Dot away. The family had a private hour before she was gone.

One of the funeral directors visited early the next morning to discuss arrangements for the memorial service. The funeral home claries a series of questions with the family. They work up a final invoice for all services so the family does not receive a series of bills.

a. Did I want a viewing? No – Let people remember her the way she was.
b. The cost for the cremation
c. Number of death certificates
d. When did I want the memorial service? I chose two weeks after her demise so friends and relations could make travel and time arrangements
e. Contribution for the pastor
f. Contribution for the organist
g. Contribution for the custodian
h. Cost of the obituary notice; I had the immediate announcement put in the area newspaper and repeated in the paper two days before the service as a reminder. I also had it listed in Dot's hometown paper.
i. They asked if I wanted funeral home personnel at the memorial service. I said.
j. No. He replied, "You saved $600". What kind or flowers did we want?
k. What kind of a book for people to sign?
l. What kind of an urn did I want? - A plain one. They returned the ashes to me five days after the cremation.
m. Was I planning an immediate burial? No
n. I asked that the obituary state in lieu of flowers, contributions be sent to Hospice.

Hospice told me those monies go to defray the expenses for others.

Hospice called all those who sent a contribution, as well as sent thank you notes.

They also sent me a list of those who contributed.

> **Tip**: *Ask the funeral home to estimate the itemized costs for services they provide.*

Return Equipment

Within an hour after the funeral director left, a crew from Hospice came and removed the bed and collected the wheelchair and walker.

Disposing of the medicine

Even though the medicine package was not opened, since I had opened the Fed Ex envelope that the medicine package was in, Hospice could not take it back. However, they took back the unopened boxes of diapers, gloves, wipes and lotions.

Notification

The next chore was to notify immediate family and friends. My son, sister and I made the calls. This was a rough assignment, but we made it through.

> **Tip**: *Prepare a list of names and telephone numbers of parties to be notified in advance if you are able.*

Memorial Service

When the date and time was established with the church for the memorial service we put the notice in the newspaper. Saturday at 2:00 pm was suitable for most people, especially those who had to travel. An 8x11 picture of Dot was placed in the church lobby for the service. The eulogies were given by the minister who officiated at our wedding, the pastor of our church, and our son, Ron, who gave a ten minute tribute to his mother. I had two gatherings after the memorial service, one at the church immediately following the service and another at the house.

>**Tip**: *Arrange for refreshments after services. I pre-ordered hamburgers to be ready to serve with drinks and cookies at the church and also catered a luncheon at home.*

Issues
Social Security

I knew Social Security had to be notified. The funeral director sends a copy of the death certificate to SS. The SS office informed me I was entitled to $255 funeral expenses. Along those lines, we had a joint bank account in which our SS checks were deposited. I was advised to keep it open for at least three months until all joint monies, and Dot's Social Security benefits were cleared.

>**Tip**: *If you receive pension benefits from an employer you must notify them if your spouse was a beneficiary on your pension plan.*
>**Tip**: *The funeral home notifies Social Security of the death of the beneficiary.*

Sympathy cards and thank you notes

For the first couple of weeks we received lots of sympathy cards. Four weeks later we were still receiving some. Many had special notes about their remembrance of Dot. It got pretty rough when the mailman came because I knew the tears would roll as I read the condolences. Likewise, as I wrote thank you cards the tears came. I was told over and over again by those who have gone through it, the Hospice counselor and pastors, that this was all part of the healing process.

For the first month when I met someone who expressed sympathy, my eyes would well up and tears would be on the brink. It occurred anytime when a strong memory came to mind.

Alone

Dot and I liked to garden together. During the warm afternoons in the spring and fall we often heard piercing shrills above our heads. We looked up to see a pair of broad wing hawks soaring high above. Not a wing in motion, they just turned slowly in the thermal as the gentle wind glided them eastward. The pair would call to each other as they soared. I would say to Dot, "Wouldn't you like to be able to do that?" On a warm sunny day a week after Dot passed away I decided to cut the lawn to get some much needed exercise. I was half way done when I heard a shrill cry over the roar of the lawn mower. I stopped the mower and looked. There high above was a lone broad wing calling out. I just stood there as tears rolled down. The welling and tears still occur when the right chord is struck, but I am learning that it is a natural thing, and not to be ashamed about your feelings.

Two months later, it is quiet, I am back doing engineering consulting, and I will continue to write my nature book. I have to start to take stock of what to do down the road.

Table of Contents

Acknowledgement iii
Introduction iv

Chapter 1 Onset of the Disease 1
    Background 1
    Alzheimer Disease 1
    Legal protection 1
    Bills 2
    Social Security, Pension taxes, Medicare 2
    Support organizations 3
    Changes 3
    Sun-downing behaviors 5
    Patient Behaviors 7
    Wedding album 8
    Denial 8
    Therapy 9
    Medication Interaction 9
    Falls 9
    Dead-weight-lift 10
    Amusements 10
    Travel 11

Chapter 2 Adjustments 15
    Appointments 15
    Assisted Living Homes 15
    Geriatric Assessment 16
    Relief for the caregiver 16
    Assistance 17
    Religious service 18

- Holidays 18
- Bed Linens 18
- Sheets 18
- Mattress cover 19
- Cleaning the house 19
- The Garden 20
- Walking 20
- Laundry 21
- Clothing 22
- Hygiene 24
- Eyes 25
- Hair 25
- Teeth 25
- Nails 26
- Toilet 26
- Groceries 26
- Setting the table 27
- Flatware 27
- Meals 28
- Preparing the meals 28
- Eating 29
- Chores 29

Chapter 3 Progression of the Disease 31
- House plants 33
- Frustration 33
- Motion detectors 33
- Bedcovers 34
- Rejection 34
- Role change 34
- Affection 35

Chapter 4 Medication 37
    1997 37
    1998 37
    2002 37
    2003 37
    2004 38
    2005 38
    2006 39

Chapter 5 Going Home 43
    Hospice 43
    Nightgown 44
    Diapers 44
    Mirror 45
    Food 45
    Calories 46
    Funeral arrangements 47
    Funeral Home 47
    Return Equipment 49
    Disposing of the medicine 49
    Notification 49
    Memorial Service 49
    Issues 50
    Social Security 50
    Sympathy cards and thank you notes 50
    Alone 51

About the Authors 57

About the Authors

Fred Buse   **Marie Louise Mayer**

Marie Mayer graduated with honors from Moravian College, in Bethlehem, Pennsylvania where she currently resides. She worked in Public Relations and Marketing at the College prior to her retirement. She is the proud mother of five successful children. During the years many interests and writing experiences prompted her first book published to benefit volunteer missionaries to Peru. She is the loving grandmother to eleven grandchildren; all have earned Masters' or Doctoral degrees. Four adorable great-grandchildren also have joined the happy family circle. A friendship with Fred Buse led to her intently interviewing him and writing the story about his caretaking journey dealing with his wife's Alzheimer disease. The tips offered are unique from his experiences while puzzling out what it takes to cope as the disease progresses. Everyone's life has a story written on the invisible ledger of eternity. Pages written by birthright; time, place, privilege, poverty, peace, war, love, hate, religion, faith, happiness, despair, health, handicap, and day by day continuous choices, until each story comes to a physical end and the ledger is read.

www.ingramcontent.com/pod-product-compliance
Lightning Source LLC
LaVergne TN
LVHW011518180325
806024LV00007B/40